USB

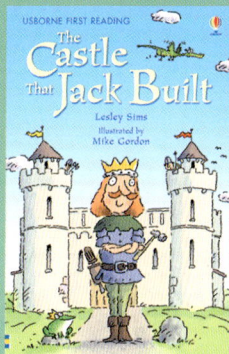
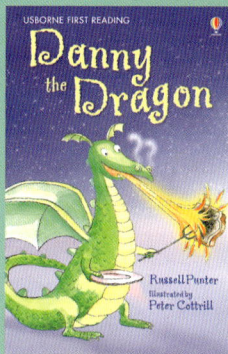
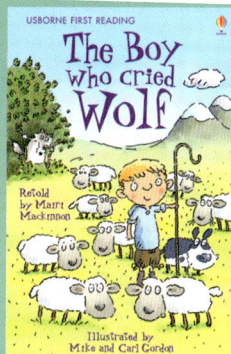

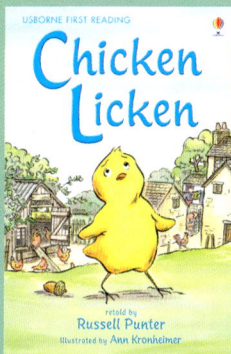

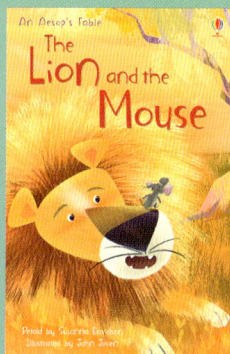

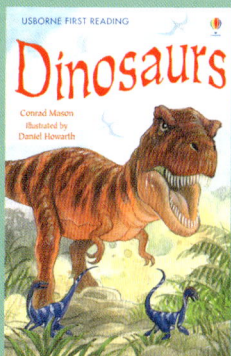
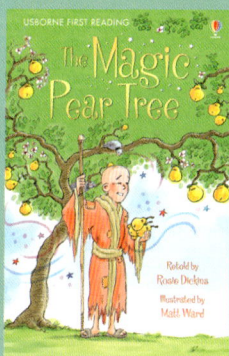
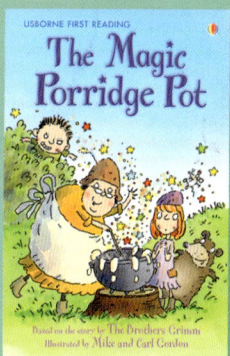

The Ant and the Grasshopper

Retold by Susanna Davidson

Illustrated by John Joven

Reading consultant: Alison Kelly

Fiddle-dee-dum!
Fiddle-dee-dee!

Riddle-dee-riddle!
Riddle-dee-dee!

sang Grasshopper.

Ant shook his head as
he hurried past.

"Don't you want to hear the rest of my song?" said Grasshopper.

"No time to stop!"
said Ant.

"I'm *busy*, *busy*, *busy*!"

"But what *are* you doing, Ant?" asked Grasshopper.

"I'm collecting food for winter," said Ant.

Ha

Ha

Ha

Ha

Ha

Ha

Grasshopper laughed
and laughed.

"Winter won't come
for ages!" scoffed
Grasshopper.

Who cares
about winter!

"But winter *will* come," said Ant. "And there'll be no food."

What will you do then, Grasshopper?

Grasshopper simply shrugged and burst into song once more.

He sang all summer.

He sang to the swifts and
the swallows.

He sang to the butterflies
and bees.

Sometimes he stopped
to watch Ant.

20

"What a waste of a summer!" thought Grasshopper.

The days grew shorter.
The nights grew longer.

First the swifts left, and
then the swallows.

"Where are you going?"
asked Grasshopper.

"To Africa," they replied,
"in search of the sun."

In the evening, a chill wind blew. The flowers dropped their petals.

The leaves fell from
the trees.

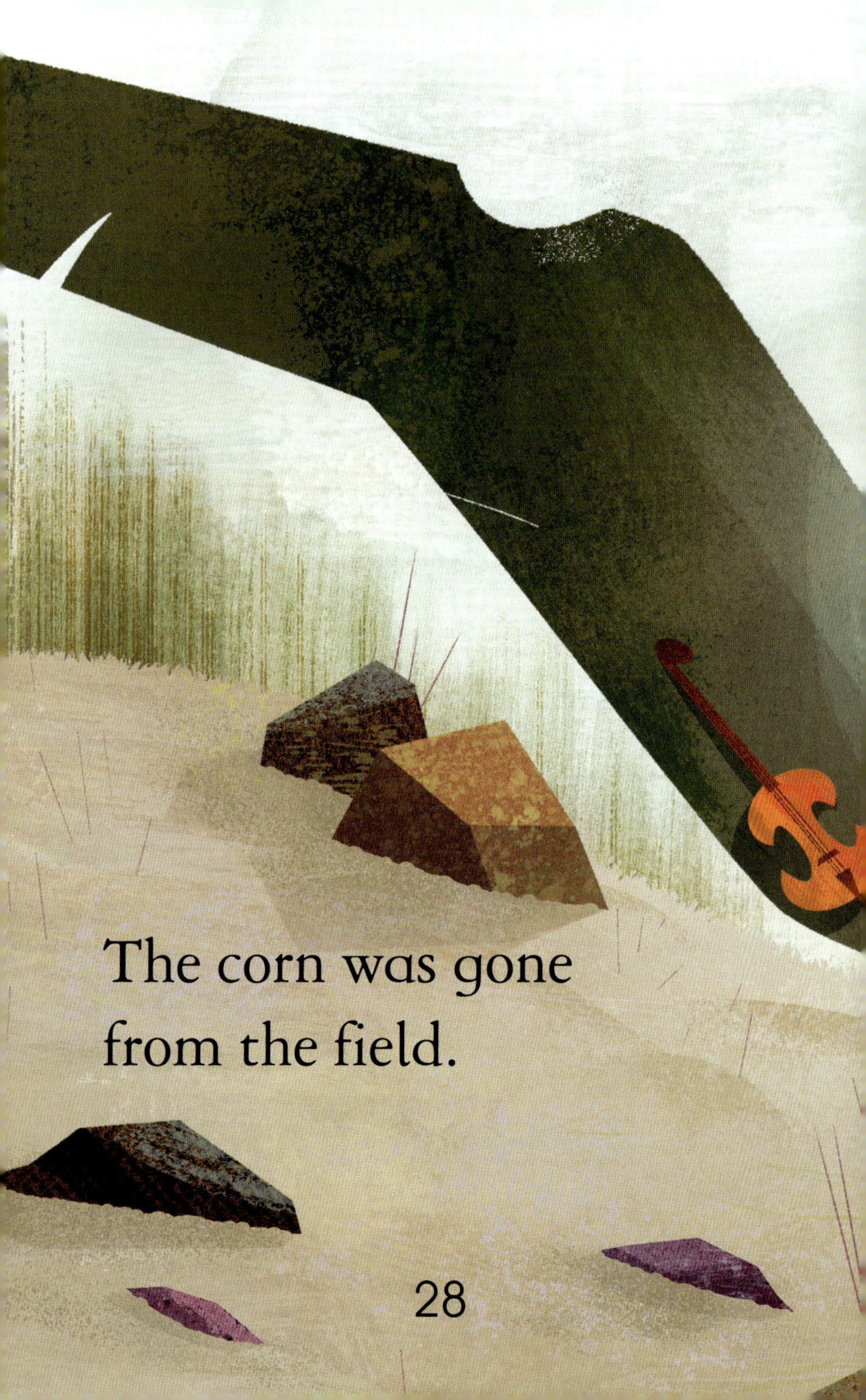

The corn was gone
from the field.

"What will I do now?"
wondered Grasshopper.

Then, one morning,
Grasshopper woke to
huge, heavy clouds.

Little white flakes danced
down to the ground.

"How beautiful!"
thought Grasshopper.

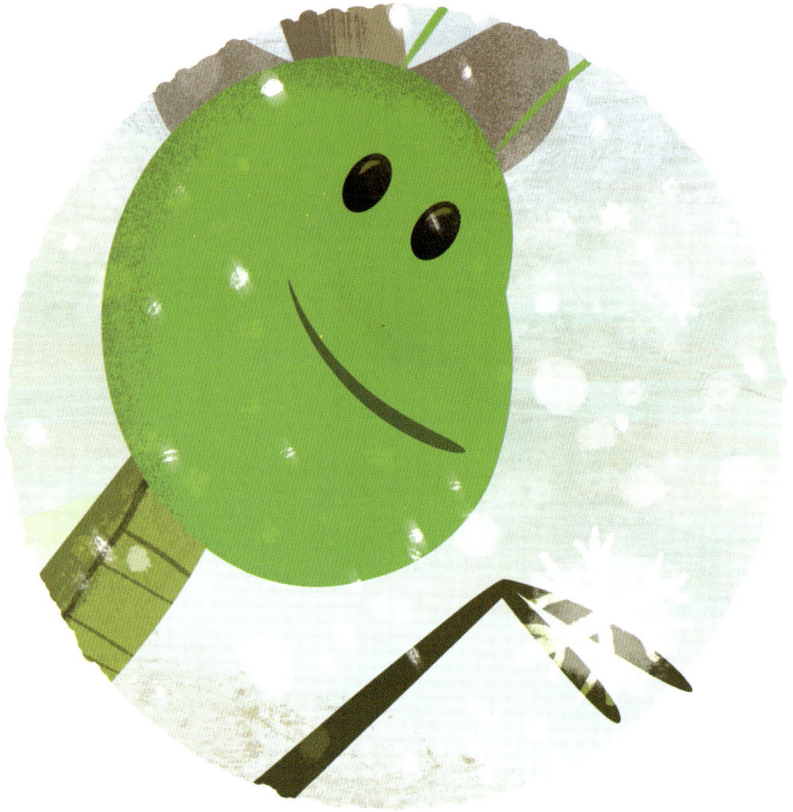

But the snow fell thick
and fast.

Grasshopper crawled
under a leaf.

He wrapped it around
himself, like a blanket.

"Ant was right!" he realized.

"I wasted my summer."

"I should have stored food for winter."

Now I have nothing.

Grasshopper closed
his eyes.

I'll just have
a little nap.

But someone, or something, was shaking him...

Wake up,
Grasshopper!
Wake up!

"You can't stay out here,
in the cold," said Ant.

"You had better come home with me."

Ant led Grasshopper underground.

Down,

down,

down they went
to his snug little home.

"Are you hungry?"
asked Ant.

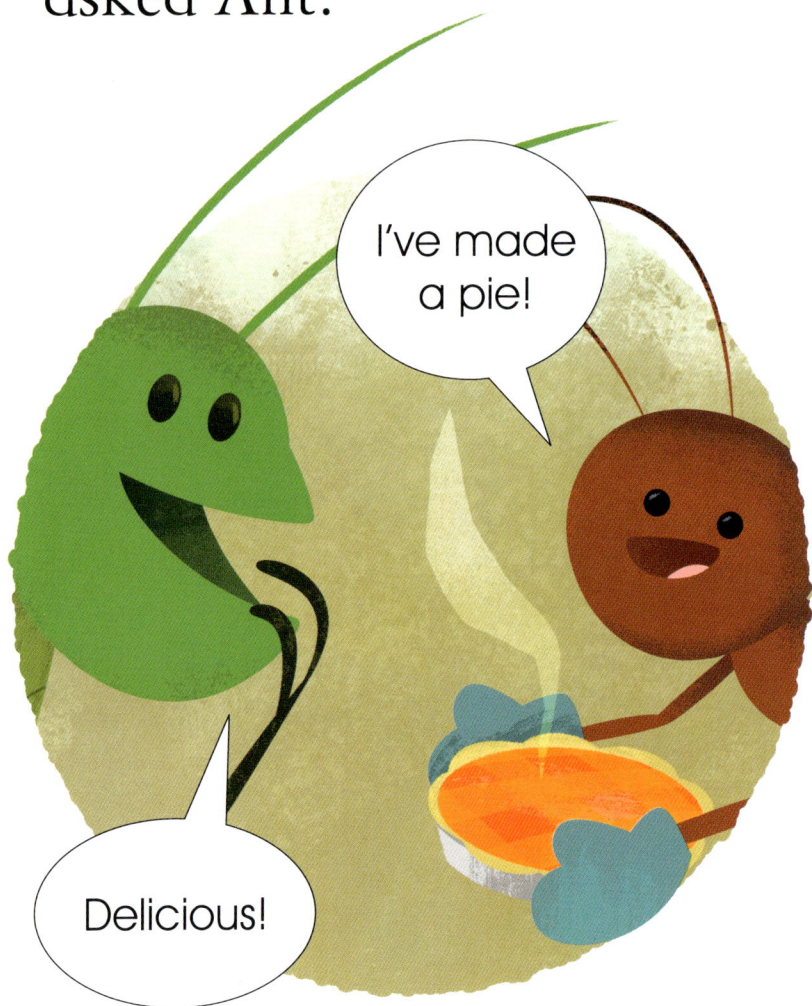

"You can stay here for the winter," said Ant. "I have food for us both."

"I'm sorry I laughed at you," said Grasshopper.

I was wrong.

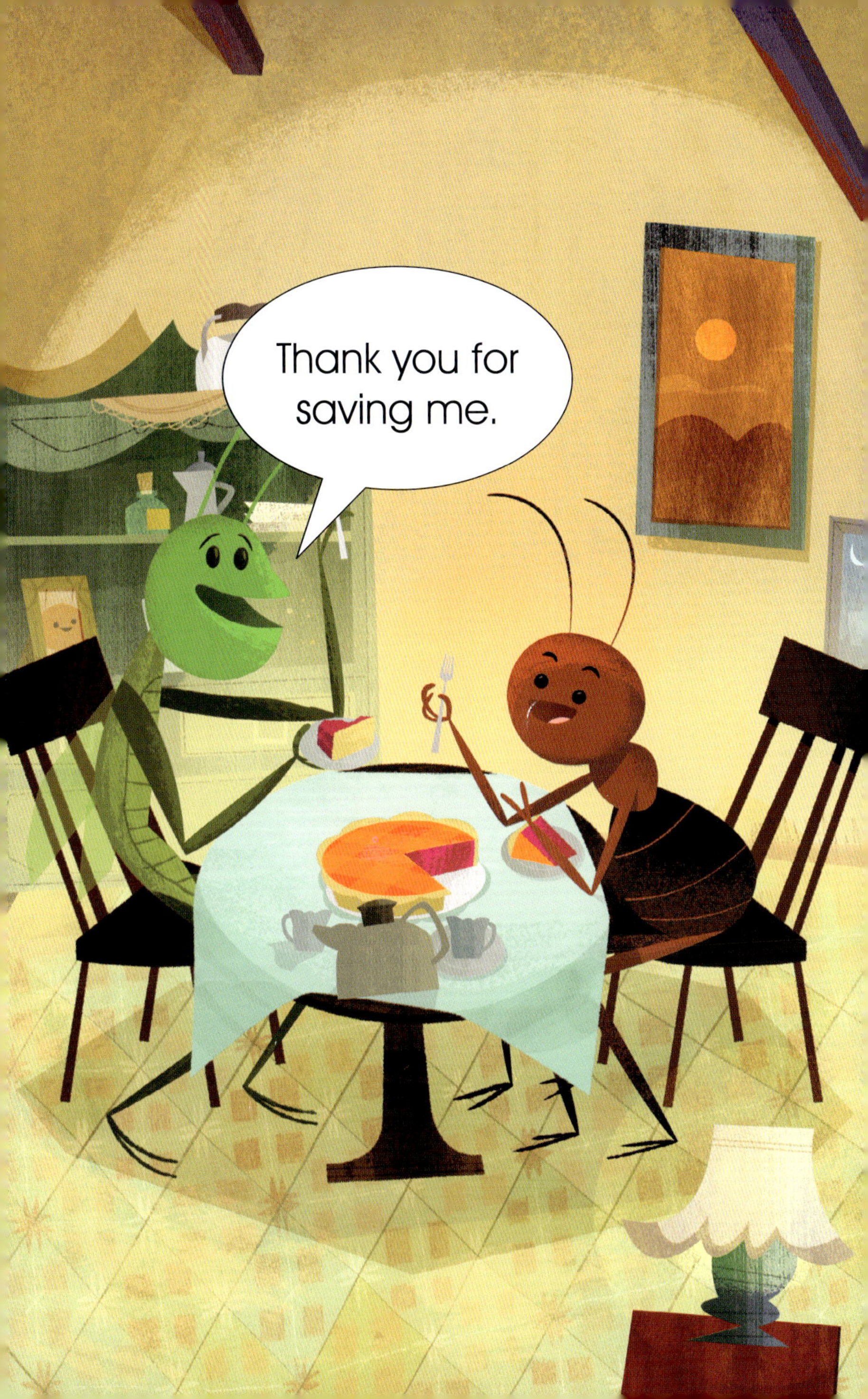
Thank you for saving me.

"I'll work next summer," Grasshopper promised.

I'll collect food for winter.

About the story

Aesop's Fables are from Ancient Greece. They always have a moral, or a lesson, at the end. The moral of this story is 'Beware of winter before it comes', or more simply, 'Be prepared'.

Designed by Vickie Robinson
Series designer: Russell Punter
Series editor: Lesley Sims

First published in 2019 by Usborne Publishing Ltd., Usborne House, 83-85 Saffron Hill, London EC1N 8RT, England. www.usborne.com Copyright © 2019 Usborne Publishing Ltd.

USBORNE FIRST READING
Level Four

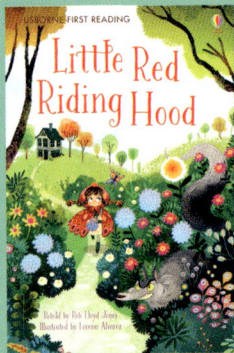

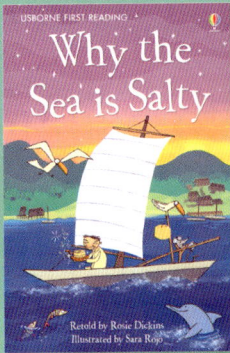

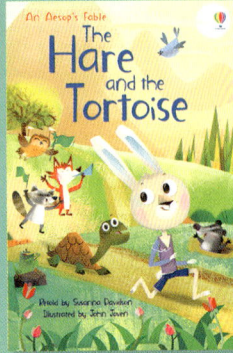

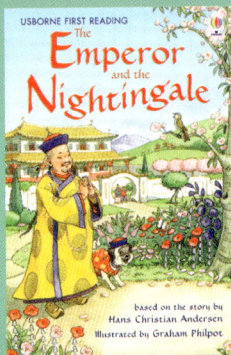

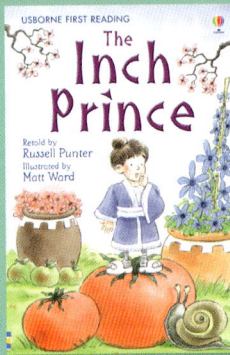

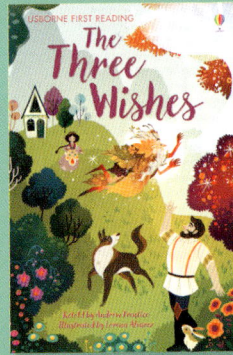

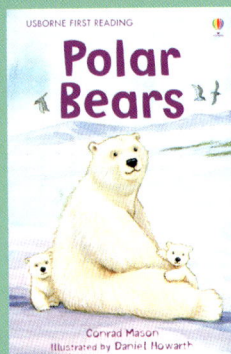

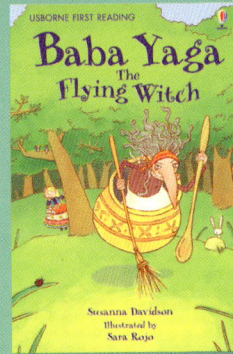

USBORNE FIRST READING

Little Red Riding Hood

Retold by Rob Lloyd Jones
Illustrated by Lorena Alvarez

USBORNE FIRST READING

Why the Sea is Salty

Retold by Rosie Dickins
Illustrated by Sara Rojo

An Aesop's Fable

The Hare and the Tortoise

Retold by Susanna Davidson
Illustrated by John Joven

USBORNE FIRST READING

The Emperor and the Nightingale

based on the story by
Hans Christian Andersen
Illustrated by Graham Philpot

USBORNE FIRST READING

The Inch Prince

Retold by Russell Punter
Illustrated by Matt Ward

USBORNE FIRST READING

The Three Wishes

Retold by Andrew Prentice
Illustrated by Lorena Alvarez

USBORNE FIRST READING

Polar Bears

Conrad Mason
Illustrated by Daniel Howarth

USBORNE FIRST READING

The Golden Carpet

Retold by M. Mackinnon
Illustrated by Alida Massari

USBORNE FIRST READING

Baba Yaga The Flying Witch

Susanna Davidson
Illustrated by Sara Rojo